Color Yourself to
INNER PEACE

AND REDUCE STRESS
WITH YOUR WINGED
ANIMAL SPIRITS

ORIGINAL ART BY **Sue Coccia**

CICO BOOKS
LONDON NEW YORK

Published in 2016 by CICO Books
An imprint of Ryland Peters & Small Ltd
20–21 Jockey's Fields   341 E 116th St
London WC1R 4BW   New York, NY 10029

www.rylandpeters.com

10 9 8 7 6 5 4 3 2 1

A CIP catalog record for this book is
available from the Library of Congress
and the British Library.

Senior editor: Carmel Edmonds
Designer: Emily Breen
Art director: Sally Powell
Head of production: Patricia Harrington
Publishing manager: Penny Craig
Publisher: Cindy Richards

US ISBN: 978-1-78249-371-6
(Color Yourself to Inner Peace)

UK ISBN: 978-1-78249-374-7
(Colour Yourself to Inner Peace)

Printed in China

Contents

About the Author

From the Andean condor to the sphinx moth, Sue Coccia has a unique relationship with winged creatures. Her love of animals developed at an early age and encouraged her to nurture and protect them. A life abundant with profound winged encounters, including holding a small hummingbird and feeding a golden eagle, has lent inspiration to create their stories through art.

Her travels as a professional artist have taken her to such places as South America, Egypt, and the Galapagos to learn more about these fascinating flying messengers. Living in a small town in the Pacific Northwest, USA, Sue draws by hand these natural wonders which we share the earth with. This has been her full-time career since 1996.

People are often drawn to her work because it makes them feel good—because she offers them symbols of luck, prosperity, and happiness. She compares drawing to meditating, and the results are as calming and soothing to her as they are to those who seek them out. Inner peace through our winged friends is the goal of this book.

It takes an interesting woman to view the world differently from the rest of us, and Sue is all of that. Diversity is another unmistakable element in her drawings, and that is an offshoot of her tiny bit of Native American background; her grandmother's grandmother was Cherokee, giving Sue a full appreciation for different cultures. She uses Native American, Polynesian, and Aboriginal images to show that we're all connected in some manner.

Sue holds memberships in an array of wildlife organizations. Among them are the Orca Network, Bats Northwest, the International Crane Foundation, and the International Wolf Center.

She is a highly disciplined person in so many ways. Sue holds a black belt in Tae Kwon Do and is a devoted gardener—an activity that gave her a strong affinity for ladybugs and her signature stroke: she incorporates a ladybug into each one of her drawings. No one sees and duplicates the world quite like Sue.

Her highly detailed artwork is in demand worldwide, from Edmonds in Washington, USA, to India, finding its way into stores, bookshops, museums, and national parks. Her colorful animal totems can be seen hanging in homes, adorning books, notecards, and blankets, and even filling up a downtown mural.

OSPREY guardian, creativity, vision

ANDEAN CONDOR
purification, vision, rebirth

SUE COCCIA

HAWK
messenger, warrior, healing

SUE COCCIA ©

GREAT HORNED OWL
wisdom, vision, insight

BALD EAGLE

connection to spirit, healing, illumination

PHOENIX rejuvenation, peace, prosperity

SUE COCCIA

FALCON *power, awareness, success*

BARN OWL

nurture, wisdom, dream time

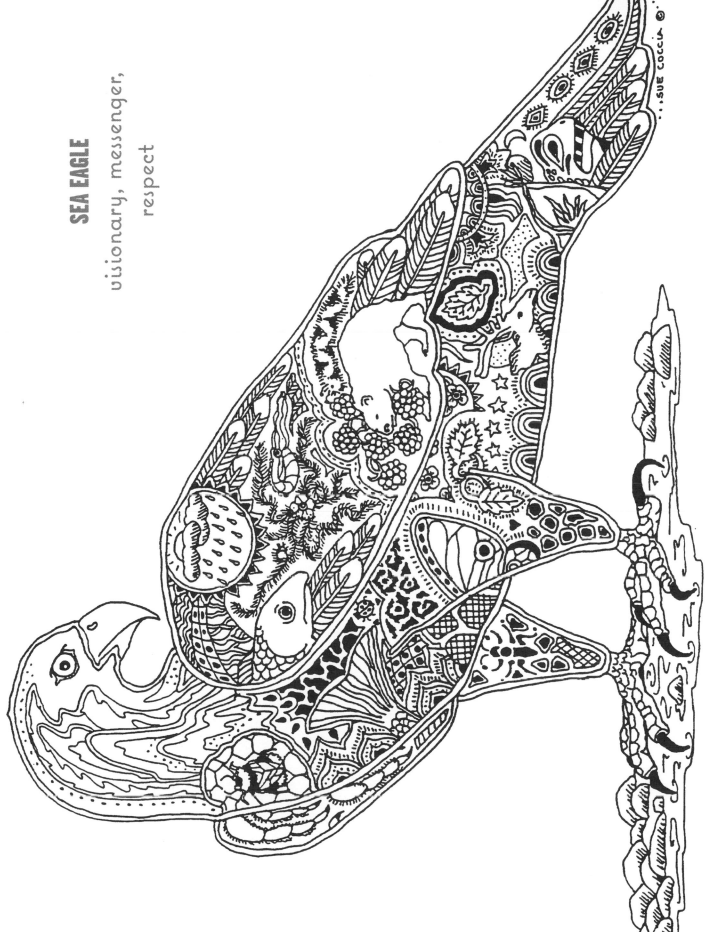

SEA EAGLE

visionary, messenger,
respect

PEACOCK BUTTERFLY
courage, good luck, transformation

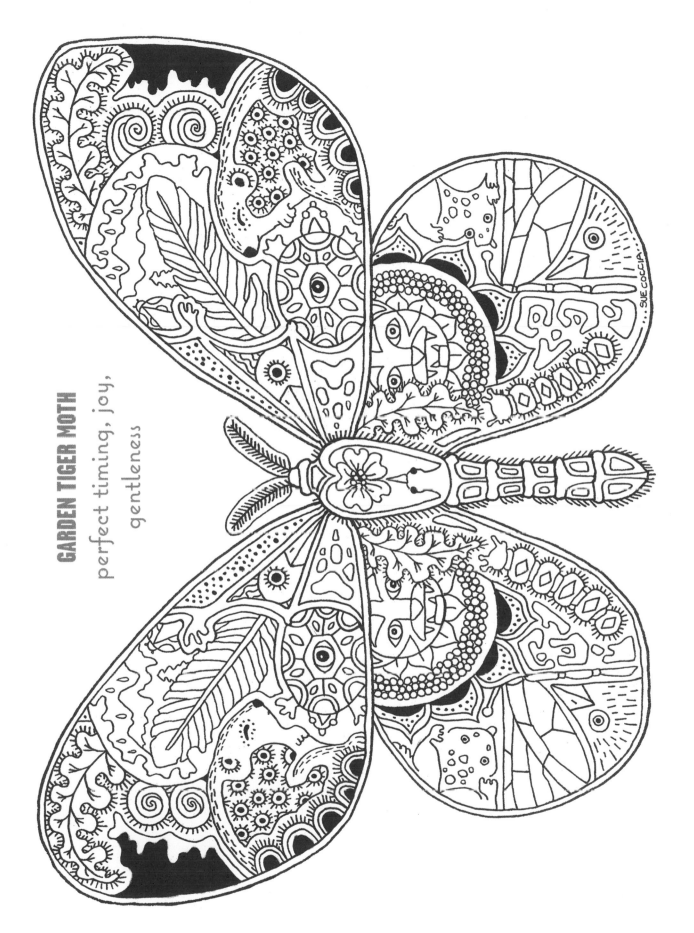

GARDEN TIGER MOTH

perfect timing, joy, gentleness

SUE COCCIA

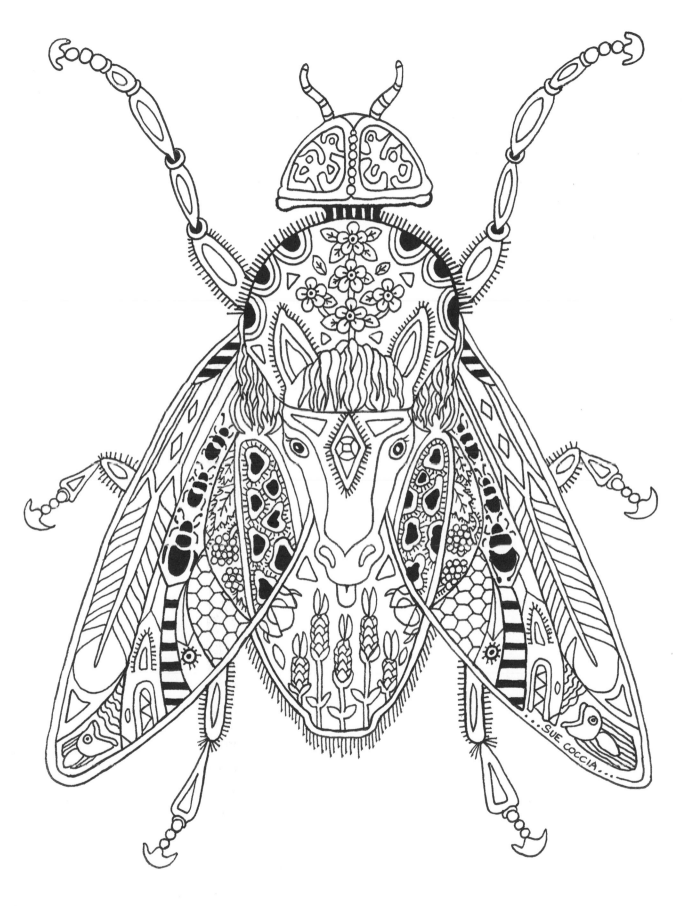

HORSEFLY change, spiritual healing, truthfulness

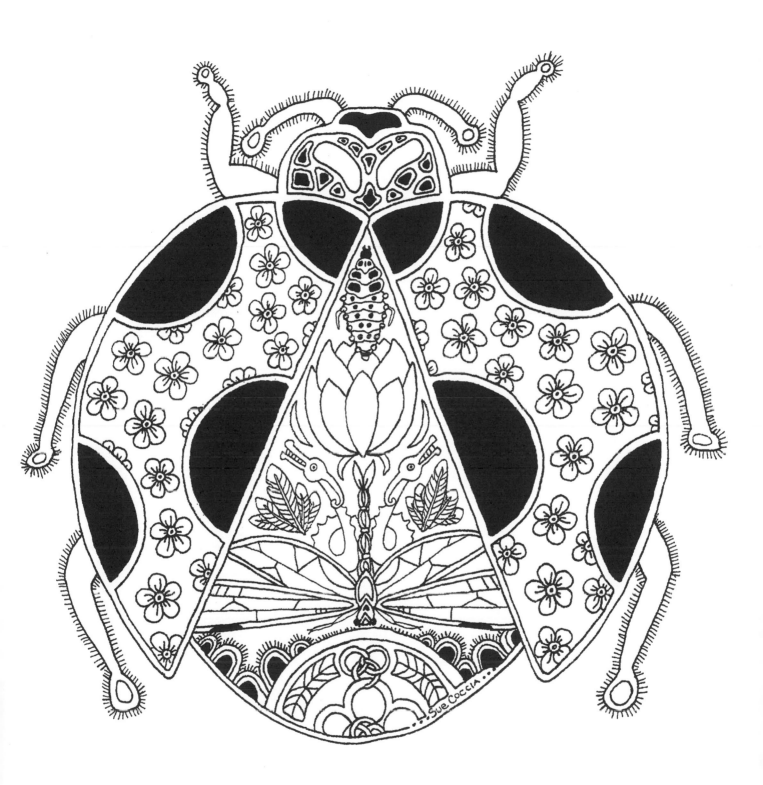

LADYBUG good luck, happiness, joy

COMMA BUTTERFLY
spiritual growth,
gentleness, loving

DRAGONFLY skill, agility, enlightenment

LUNA MOTH

sensitivity, dreaming, intuition

...SUE COCCIA Ⓒ...

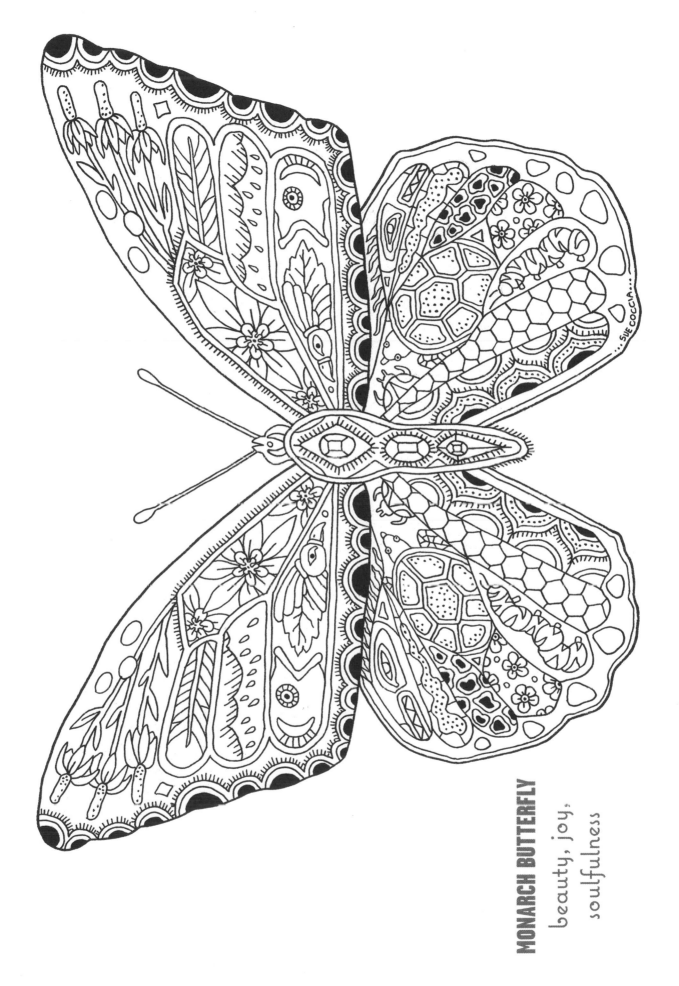

MONARCH BUTTERFLY

beauty, joy, soulfulness

SPHINX MOTH

courage, perception, intuition

... SUE GOCCIA ...

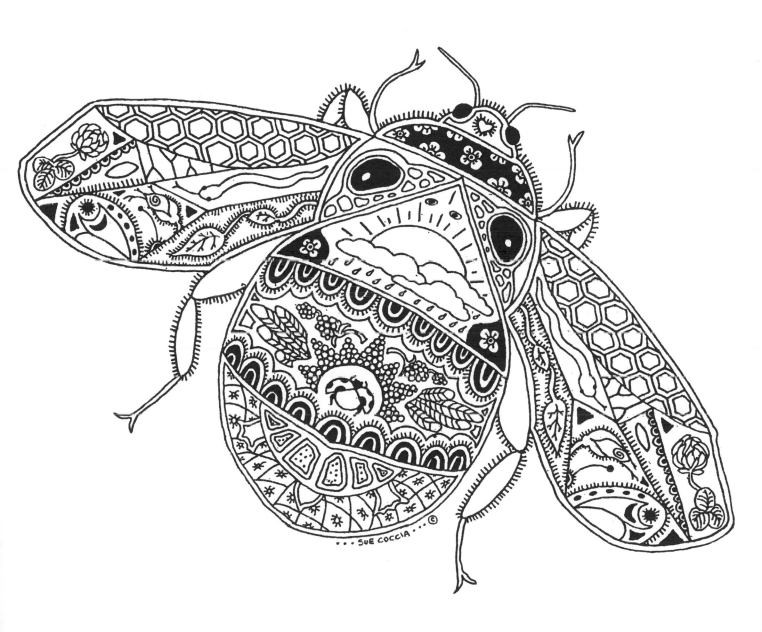

... SUE COCCIA ... ©

BEE productivity, harmony, bliss

BLUE MORPHO BUTTERFLY

freedom of spirit, balance, grace

SUE COCCIA

POLISH CHICKEN
fertility, new growth,
balance

for Henry

OSTRICH

cleansing, meditation, grounding

SUE COCCIA

WOODPECKER protection, communication, fertility

PTARMIGAN loyalty, innocence, agility

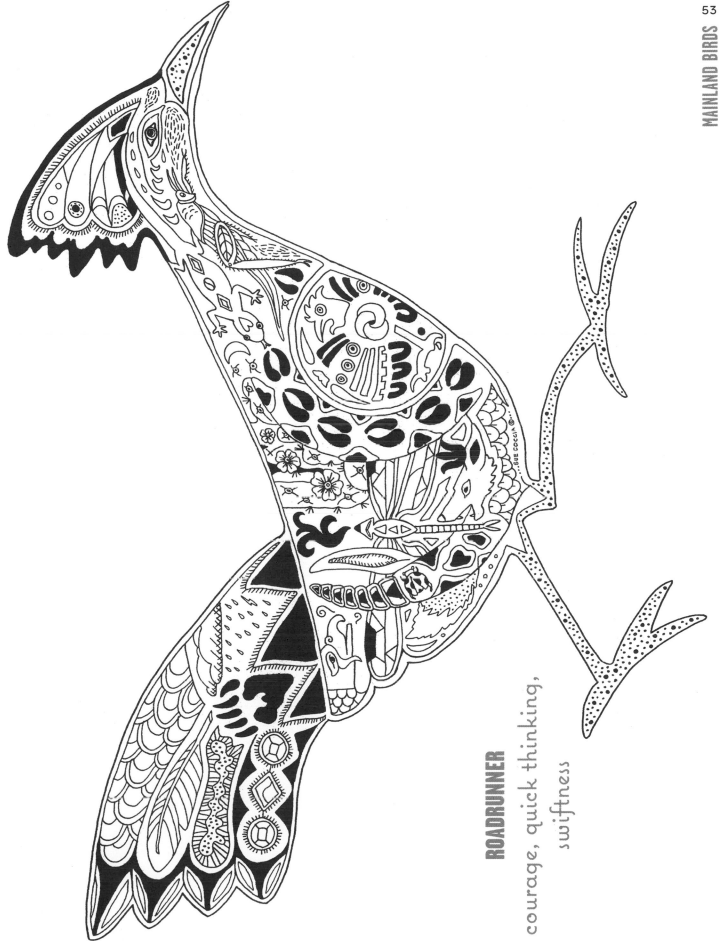

ROADRUNNER
courage, quick thinking, swiftness

CHICKADEE joy,
cheerfulness, truth

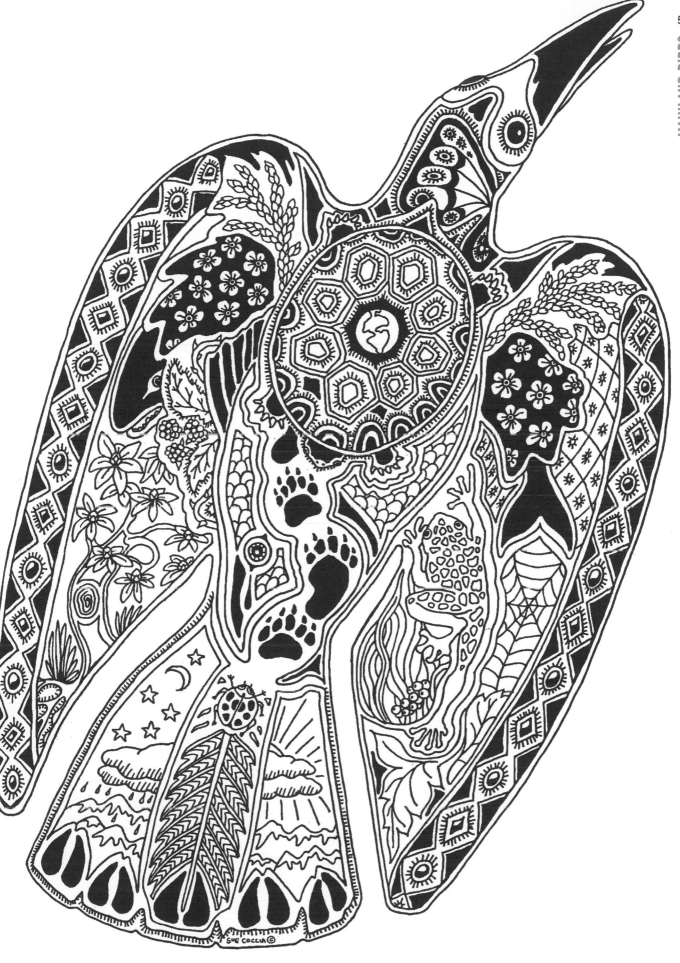

RAVEN transformation, rebirth, playfulness

STELLER'S JAY

potential, grounding, energy

ROOSTER drama, good reputation, watchfulness

PIGEON

love, security, peace

...SUE COCCIA...

PELICAN generosity, resilience, open heart

LOON

serenity, communication, stillness

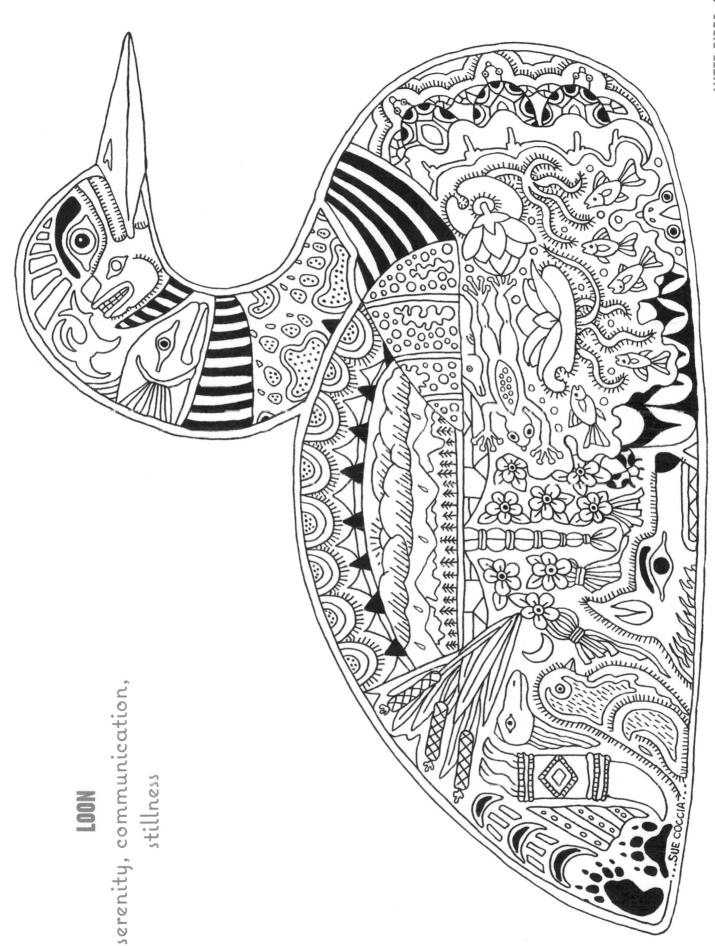

...SUE COCCIA...

CRANE longevity, focus, protection

KINGFISHER abundance, success, new ventures

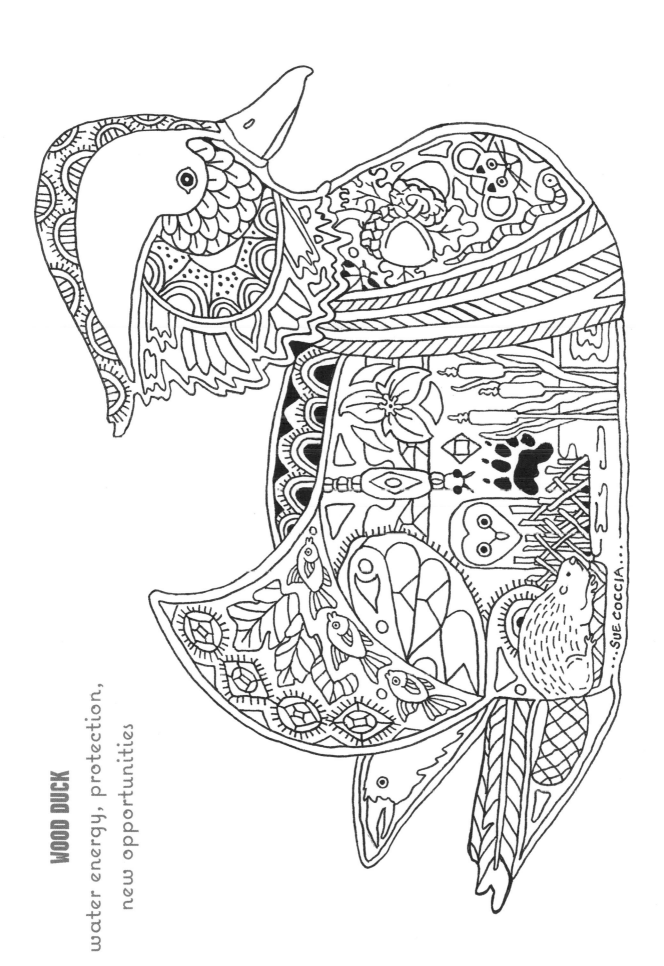

WOOD DUCK

water energy, protection,
new opportunities

...SUE COCCIA...

GREAT BLUE HERON

grounding, boundaries,
sanctity

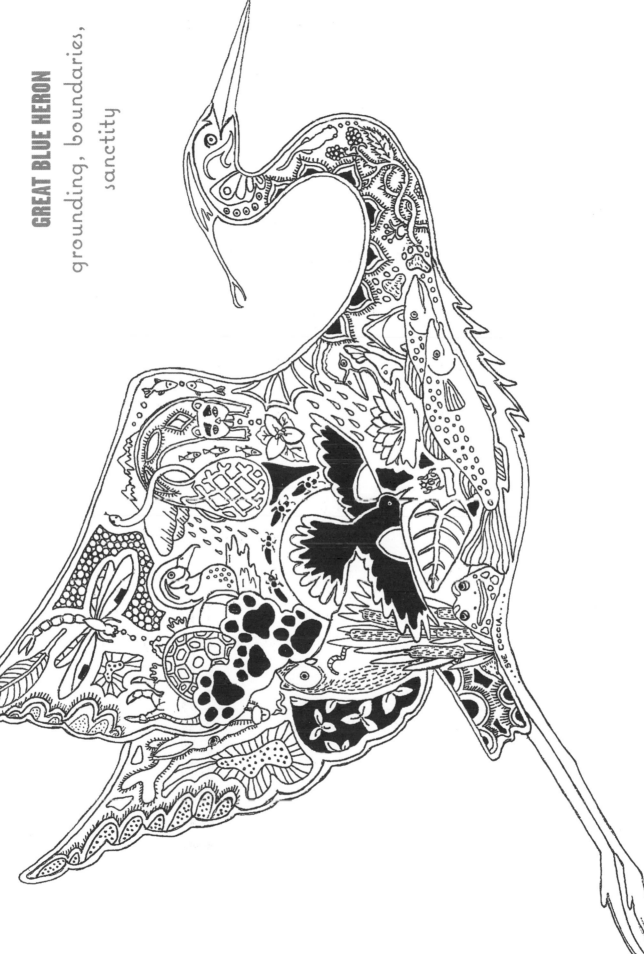

SPOONBILL

strength, higher
knowledge, energy

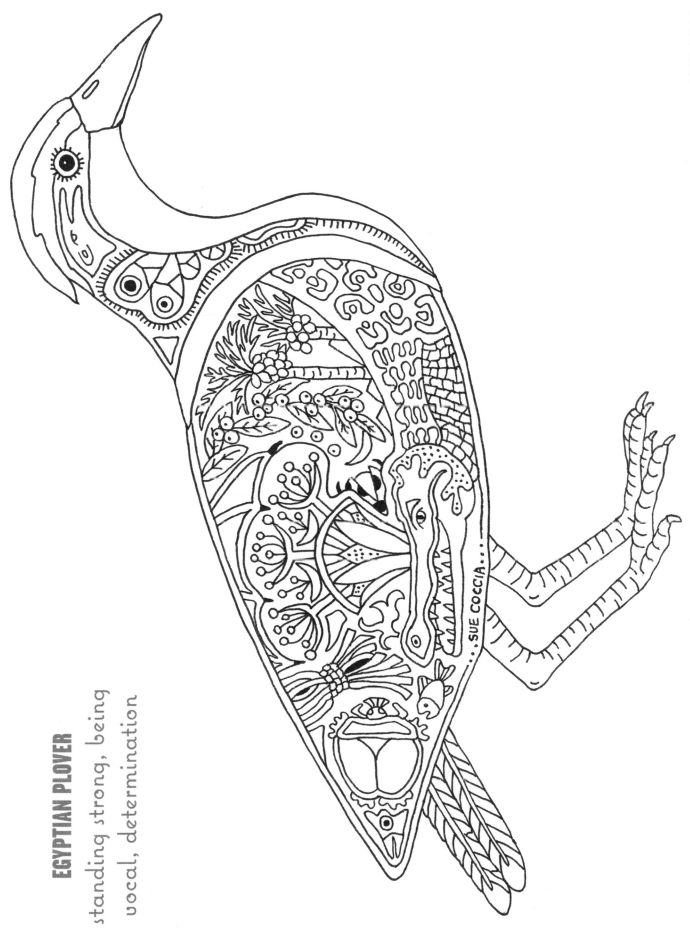

EGYPTIAN PLOVER

standing strong, being
vocal, determination

...SUE COCCIA...

CANADA GOOSE *love of home, affection, intuition*

...SUE COCCIA...

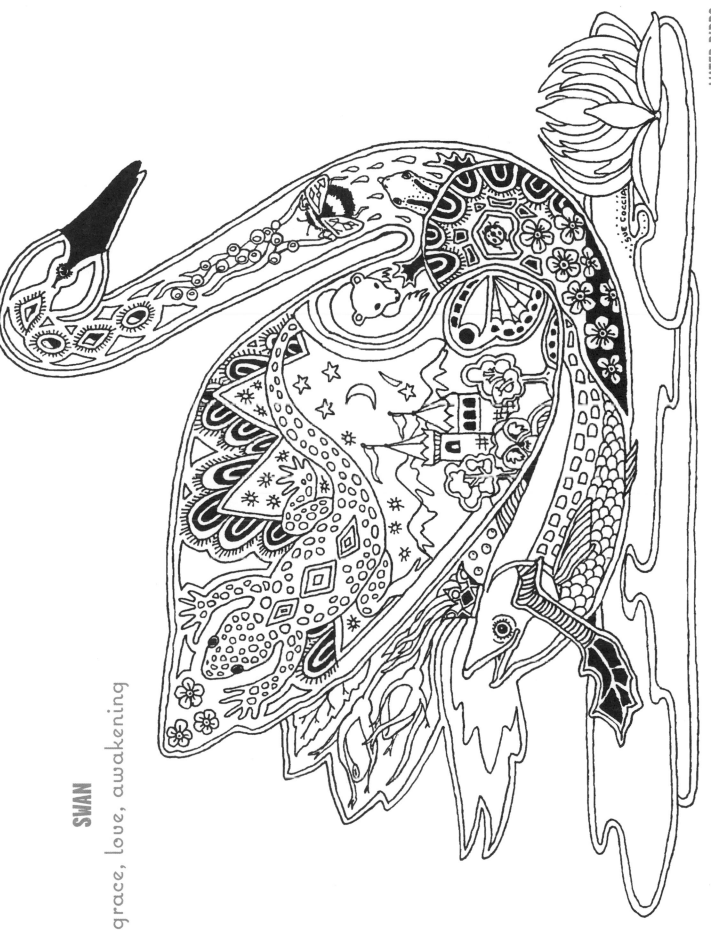

SWAN

grace, love, awakening

FLAMINGO

journey afar,
strength, cleansing

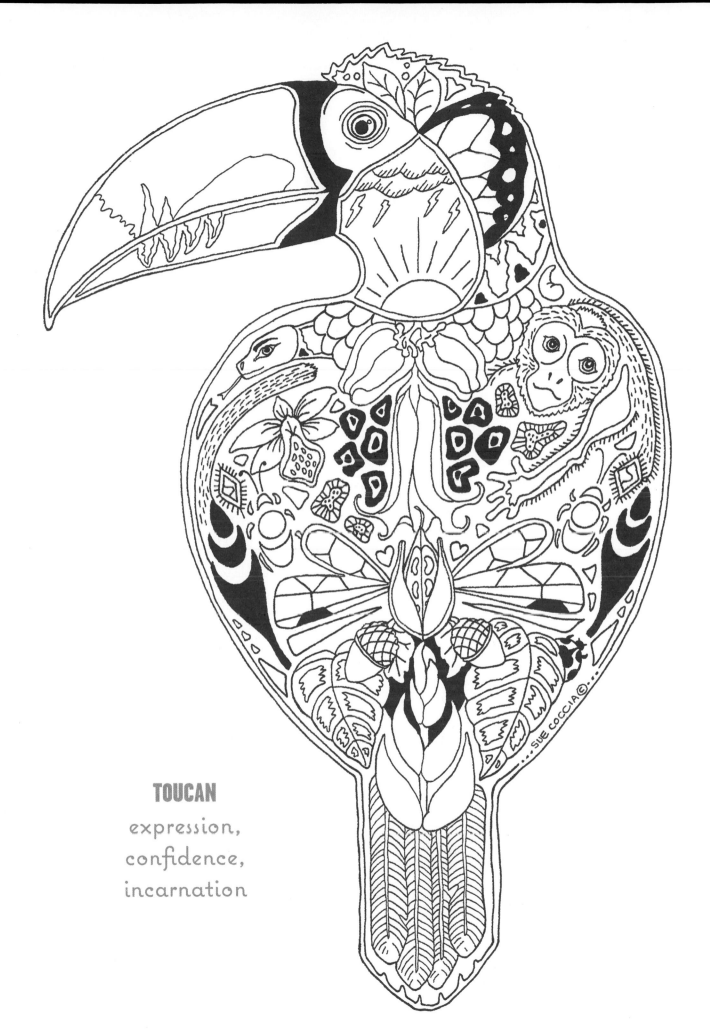

TOUCAN

expression,
confidence,
incarnation

PEACOCK
beauty,
self-assurance,
renewal

SUE COCCIA

... SUE COCCIA ...

RESPLENDENT QUETZAL magic, survivor, elegance

SUE COCCIA ©

MACAW creativity, perception, sociability

HUMMINGBIRD
joy, magic, beauty